DK WORKBOOKS

pre-K Geography

Author Mark Shulman
Educational Consultant Kara Pranikoff

Editors Jolyon Goddard,
Cecile Landau, Rohini Deb,
Nancy Ellwood, Margaret Parrish
Art Editor Tanvi Nathyal
Assistant Art Editor Kanika Kalra
Managing Editor Soma B. Chowdhury
Managing Art Editors Richard Czapnik,
Ahlawat Gunjan
Producer, Pre-Production Ben Marcus
Producer Christine Ni
DTP Designer Anita Yadav

First American Edition, 2015
Published in the United States by DK Publishing
345 Hudson Street, New York, New York 10014

Copyright © 2015 Dorling Kindersley Limited
A Penguin Random House Company
10 9 8 7 6 5
005–271679–Mar/2015

A catalog record for this book
is available from the Library of Congress.
ISBN: 978-1-4654-2851-6

DK books are available at special discounts when purchased
in bulk for sales promotions, premiums, fund-raising, or
educational use. For details, contact: DK Publishing Special
Markets, 345 Hudson Street, New York, New York 10014
SpecialSales@dk.com

Printed and bound in Hong Kong

All images © Dorling Kindersley Limited
For further information see: www.dkimages.com

A WORLD OF IDEAS
SEE ALL THERE IS TO KNOW

Contents

This chart lists all the topics in the book. Once you have completed each page, stick a star in the correct box below.

Geography is about the world and the way we use it. People who study geography are called geographers. Geographers study natural things, such as mountains and rivers. They also study things that people have added to the world, such as bridges and roads.

Look at the pictures below of four things a geographer might study. Say their names aloud. Circle the two pictures that show natural things.

bridge   mountains

river   road

The planet we live on is called Earth. It is round like a ball. Earth moves around the sun. The sun provides Earth with heat and light.

Point to each picture below of things that you find on Earth. Say the name aloud as you point.

volcano

buildings

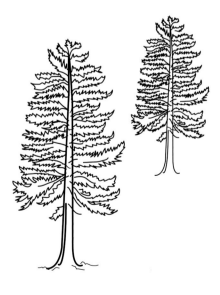

trees

island

Earth and the Solar System

Earth is a planet that moves around our sun. Other planets also move around our sun. The sun and the planets that travel around it make up our solar system.

Here is a picture of our solar system.
Earth is the third planet from the sun.
Find Earth and circle it.

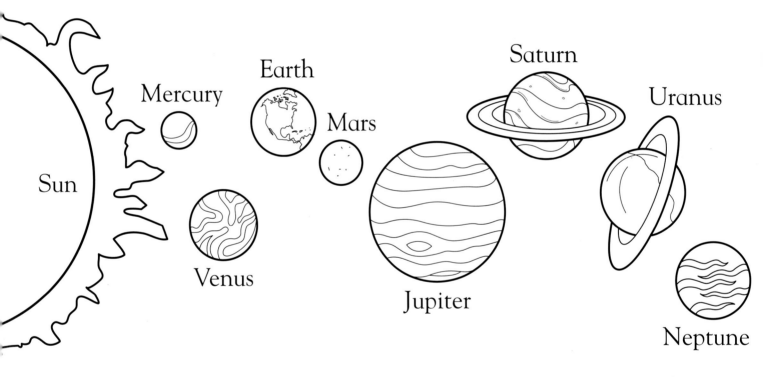

Now, count all the planets in our solar system.

How many planets are there?
Write the number in the box.

A globe is a map of planet Earth. It is shaped like a ball, just like Earth. This shape is called a sphere. A globe gives a very real picture of what our planet looks like.

Look at the picture below. How many globes and spheres can you spot? Point to each of them and say the word "globe" or "sphere" aloud.

Looking at a Globe

FACTS

A globe is made to look just like our planet Earth. Like Earth, it is a sphere. On the outside of a globe are pictures of all the land and water on Earth. Globes are often made so that they can spin around. That's because Earth spins around in space.

On this globe, draw an arrow that goes from one side of Earth to the other. Then stand up and spin around in a complete circle, just like Earth does every day!

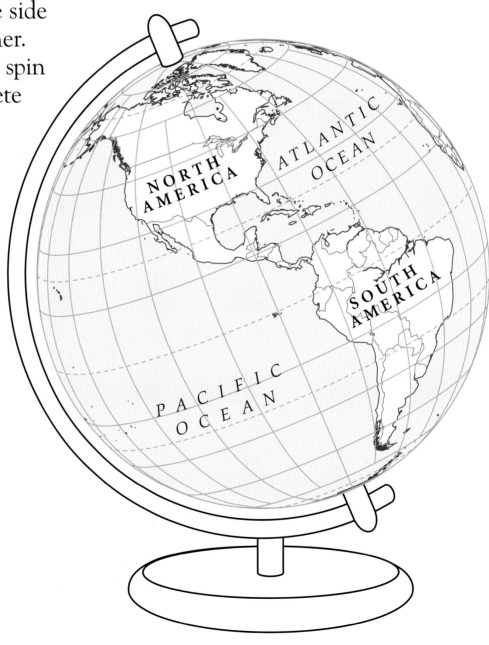

A map is a kind of picture that shows you how to get to a place and find your way around it. Globes are maps that have the same shape as Earth. But you can also use a flat map to show places on Earth. Flat maps are easier to hold and use than a globe. You can look at a flat map on paper or on a screen.

Look at the pictures below. Point to each one and say if it is a flat map or a globe.

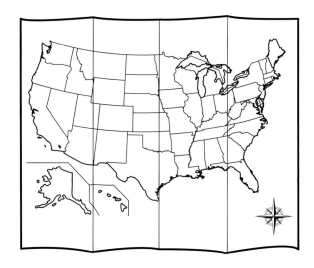

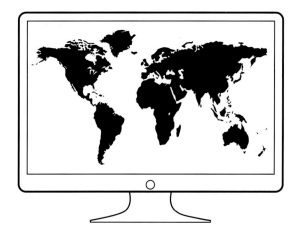

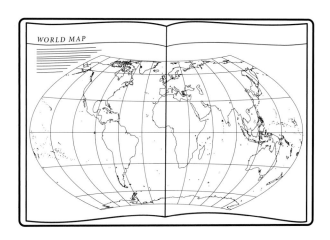

★ Types of Map

There are many different types of map. This is because we use different maps for different reasons. If you were going on a hike in a nature park, you would need a map of the park. If you wanted to know the way around your neighborhood, you would need a map of your neighborhood.

Point to the map shown below that you would use to:

1. see the real shape of Earth

2. find the best road to your friend's house

3. find buried treasure

4. find your way around a nature park

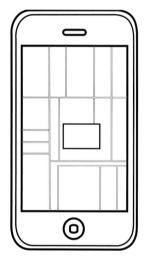

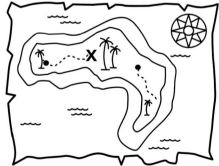

Ask an adult to show you a real map. Name some things you see on this map.

Directions

Directions are instructions that tell you where places or things are located. Using directions with a map can tell you exactly how to get from one place to another.

Look at the picture below. The cat, the dog, and the bird each have to go in a different direction to reach the house. Use your finger to trace a path from each animal to the house. Use one of the words in the box to describe the direction each animal takes.

up

across

down

★ Up and Down

FACTS

"Up" and "down" are direction words that can tell you where something is, or where something is going. When something goes up, it moves to a higher place. When something goes down, it moves to a lower position.

Look at the picture of the house above. Read the sentences below. Circle "UP" or "DOWN" to say whether the object in each sentence is UPstairs or DOWNstairs.

The bathtub is UP / DOWN.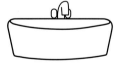

The cat is UP / DOWN.

The round table is UP / DOWN.

"In" and "out" are direction words that can tell you where you may put something or find something. You may put your books and pencils into a backpack so you can carry them to school. In class, you may take them out of your backpack so you can use them.

Draw lines from the backpack to the things that you can carry in it. Put an X (✗) over the objects that you cannot carry in the backpack.

FACTS

"Near" and "far" are direction words that tell you whether things are close together or not. Your pillow, for example, is usually near your bed but far from the bathtub. Remember that "near" and "far" can describe a very wide range of different distances. You may say that you live far from your friend. But if you think about how far you both are from the moon, you really live very near each other!

Look at the picture of the classroom above.
Draw a circle around something that is near the table.
Look out the window. Cross out something that is far away.
Draw a circle around the child who is near the window.

"Above" and "below" are direction words that are used to tell you whether something is higher or lower than another thing. Birds in the trees, for example, are above your head, while worms in the dirt are below your feet. Also, you are above the worms and below the birds.

Look at the picture above. Then circle "ABOVE" or "BELOW" to complete these sentences.

The teddy bear is ABOVE / BELOW the car.

The drum is ABOVE / BELOW the robot.

The castle is ABOVE / BELOW the airplane.

"Left" and "right" are direction words that you use based on where you are standing. If something is on the same side of you as your right hand, you say it is on your right. Something on the same side of you as your left hand is on your left.

Pretend it is you in the picture below. Hold up both your thumbs and point your fingers as shown. Put an **L** in the box next to the animals that are on your left. Put an **R** in the box next to the animals that are on your right.

left   right

Neighborhood Directions

You can use direction words to tell visitors how to reach your house and find their way around your neighborhood.

Walk around your neighborhood with an adult. Try and describe the route you take, using as many different direction words as you can remember.

Next, stand outside the front door of your home or building. Say what you see when you:

1. look up   **3.** look to the right
2. look to the left   **4.** look down

Draw one of the things you saw outside your door in the box below.

You will also need to be familiar with direction words when following or describing a route on a map.

Look at this map of a playground. Then draw arrows on the map to show the route, described below, that Buster the dog takes when he visits the playground.

1. Buster enters the playground. He runs straight ahead to the slide.

2. Buster climbs up the ladder, then goes down the slide.

3. Buster turns to his right and rushes over to the fountain, where he drinks some water.

4. Finally, Buster turns left and walks toward the tree.

Most maps have something called a compass rose. Four main directions are marked on a compass rose: "north," "south," "east," and "west." On most maps, the direction "north" is at the top and the direction "south" is at the bottom.

Here is the compass rose. Look at the letters on it.

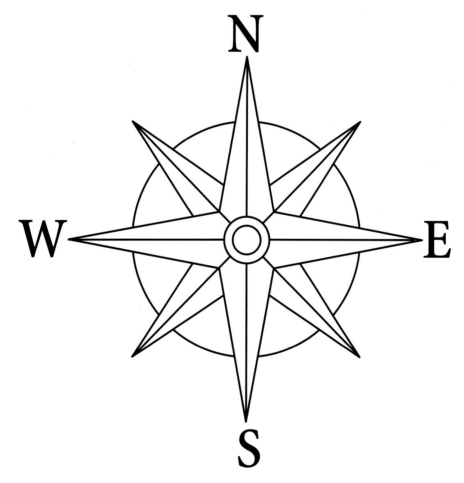

N is for north. Point to the letter **N** on the compass rose.

E is for east. Point to the letter **E** on the compass rose.

S is for south. Point to the letter **S** on the compass rose.

W is for west. Point to the letter **W** on the compass rose.

FACTS

The direction "north" is usually at the top of a map.

Here is a map of a city neighborhood. Put your finger on the fire department and move it in the direction of north. **Hint**: You are going north on the map when you move in the direction of NORTH on the compass rose.

Point to the building north of the fire department and say what it is.

The direction "south" is usually at the bottom of a map.

Look at the map of a bedroom below. Put your finger on the south wall. Say what piece of furniture is next to this wall. **Hint**: You are going south on the map when you move in the direction of SOUTH on the compass rose.

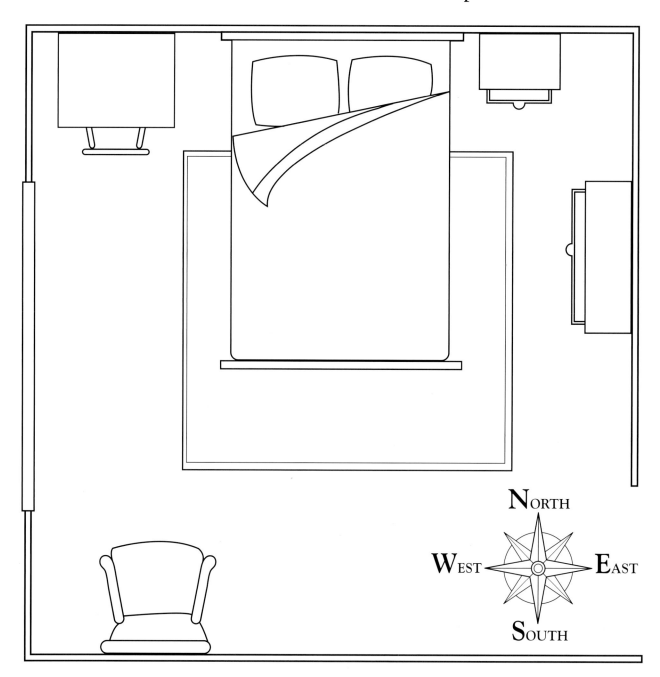

FACTS

The direction "east" is usually on the right side of a map.

Here is a map of a lake. You are helping the fish find its way. Can you say which animal is east of the fish?

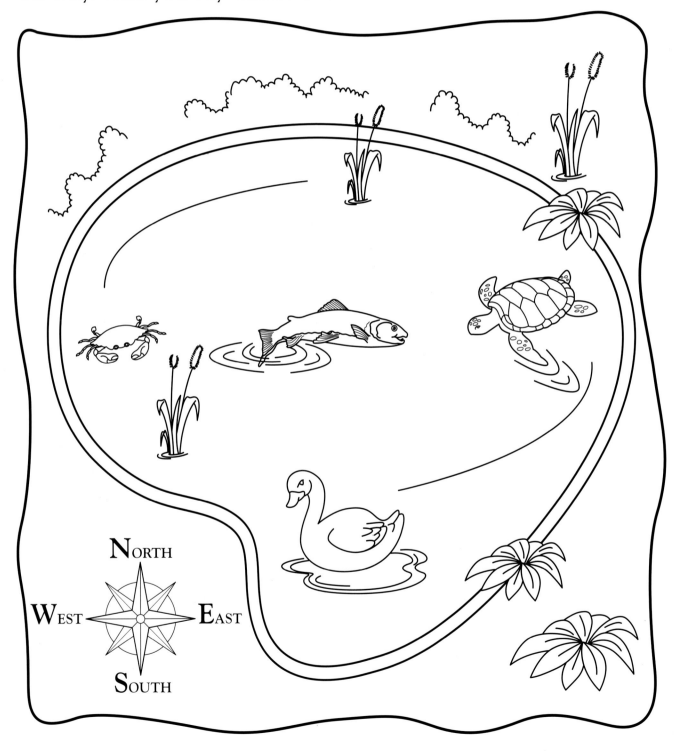

The direction "west" is usually on the left side of a map.

Here is a map of a zoo showing the animals that live there. Say which animal you will find to the west of the main building.

There are two different ways to think about the world. People study the natural world, and they also study the human world. Animals, plants, land, and water are all part of the natural world. They were on the planet before people started adding things to the world.

Here is a picture of a beach. Color the things that are part of the natural world. Circle the things that are part of the human world.

People create all kinds of things to make their lives easier. They construct roads and bridges to help them cross rivers and mountains. They build towns and cities, where they live. Anything made by people is part of the human world.

Mountains are high areas of land. A group of mountains together is called a mountain range.

Look at this map of the continent of North America. Circle the three mountain ranges that you see on it.

ARCTIC OCEAN

North America

Brooks Range

Rocky Mountains

Appalachian Mountains

ATLANTIC OCEAN

PACIFIC OCEAN

Say whether you live in the mountains or on flat land.

Forests are places with lots of trees. The trees give forest animals food and protection. The animals eat leaves, nuts, berries, and seeds. They may climb the trees and hide in the branches or dig holes to stay safe.

Circle all the forest animals you can find.

The driest places on Earth are called deserts. Deserts get very little rain. That is why you will not find very many plants growing in a desert.

You are going on vacation to a desert, where the sun is always shining. It gets very hot. Circle the things you will want to pack for your trip. Put an X (✗) on the items that you would not pack.

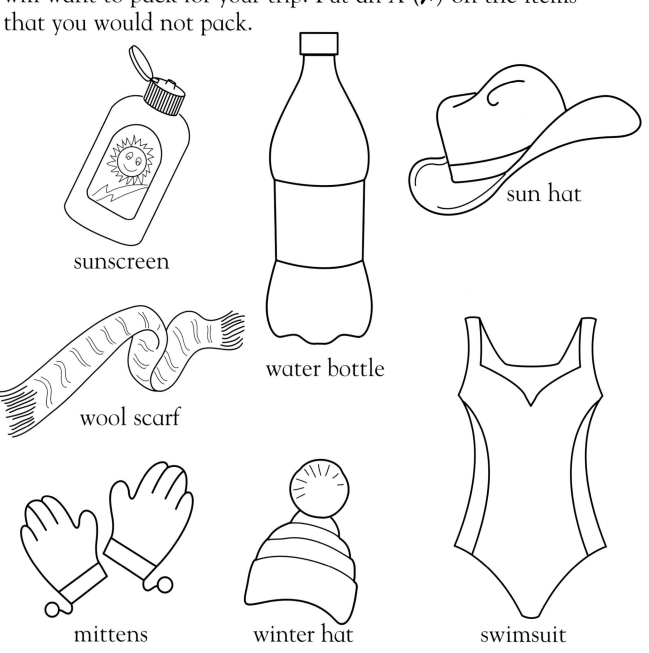

sunscreen

water bottle

sun hat

wool scarf

mittens

winter hat

swimsuit

An island is a piece of land that is surrounded by water. Islands look like they are floating in water, but they are not. Islands are the tops of mountains, most of which are under the water.

The map below shows the main islands of the state of Hawaii in the United States. Count them, then say how many there are. Color in the largest island.

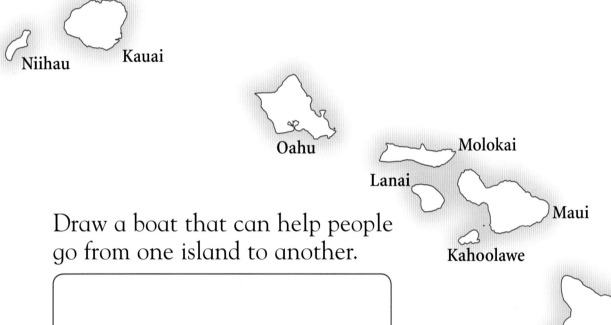

Niihau   Kauai

Oahu

Lanai

Molokai

Maui

Kahoolawe

Draw a boat that can help people go from one island to another.

Hawaii

An ocean is a very, very large body of water. Did you know that oceans take up more space on Earth than land? There are five oceans. They cover most of our planet. It is hard to see where one ocean starts and the other ends, because all oceans touch one another.

Look at the map below. Circle the names of the five oceans. Then answer the questions that follow.

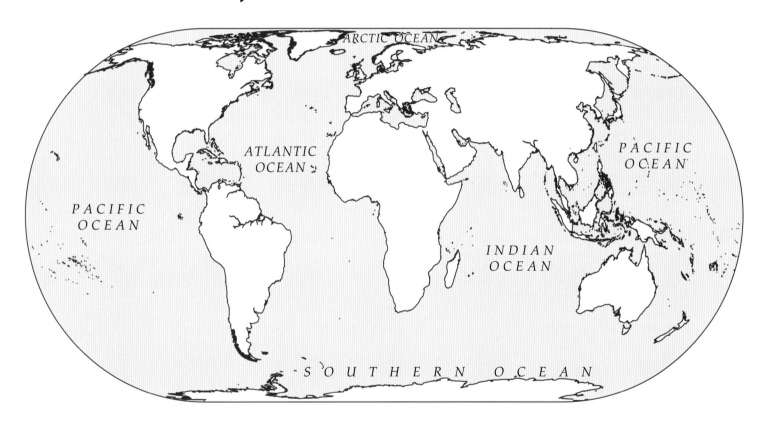

The names of two oceans begin with the same letter. Which letter is that?

Which ocean is closest to where you live?
Ask an adult to help you.

A lake is a body of water surrounded by land. Lakes are much smaller than oceans. People like to live around lakes, where they can fish, swim, and go boating.

The pictures below show different things you might use to cross a lake. Point to each one and say its name aloud. Have you used any of these to cross a lake?

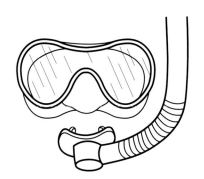

goggles and snorkel

sailboat

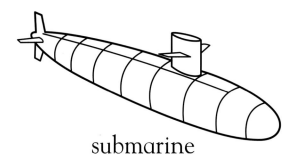

submarine

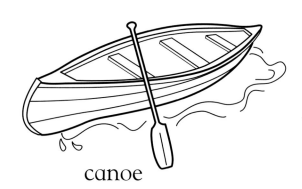

swimming float

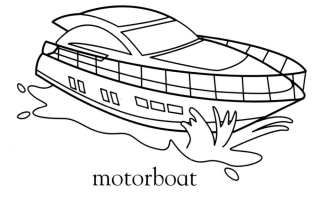

motorboat

canoe

★ | Rivers

A river is a body of water that moves from a high place to a low place. Often rivers run down the sides of mountains. Many people and animals live near rivers.

In this picture, find five living things that are using the river. Point to them and say their names aloud.

There are seven very large areas of land on Earth. These large areas of land are called continents. Asia is the largest continent. Australia is the smallest continent. Antarctica is covered with ice all year round.

Here is a flat map of the world. Color in all of the land.
Remember: Everything you do not color on this map is water.

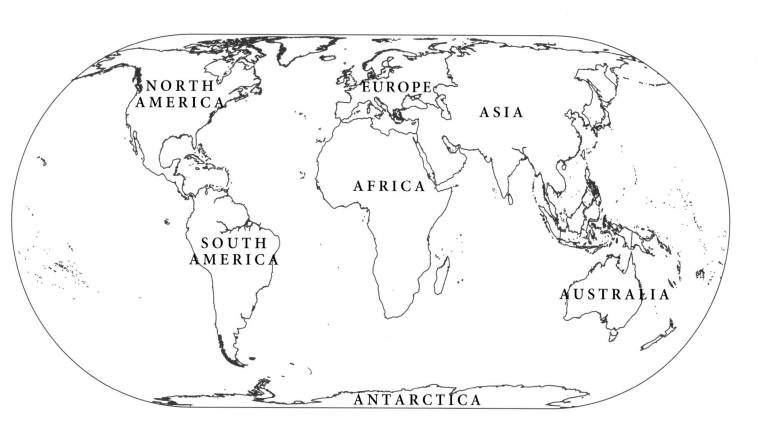

Point to the continent where you live on the map. Say its name aloud. You can ask an adult for help.

★ Countries

FACTS

Continents are divided into places called countries.
Continents are part of the natural world, but countries
are part of the human world.

Look at this map of the world.
Then answer the questions below.
Ask an adult to help you.

What is the name of the
country where you live?

....

Can you find it on
the world map?
Point to it and say
the name aloud.

Can you point to Canada
and Russia on the map?
Circle them.

Countries can be large or small. People living in the same country have the same leaders and the same flag. The two largest countries on Earth are Russia and Canada.

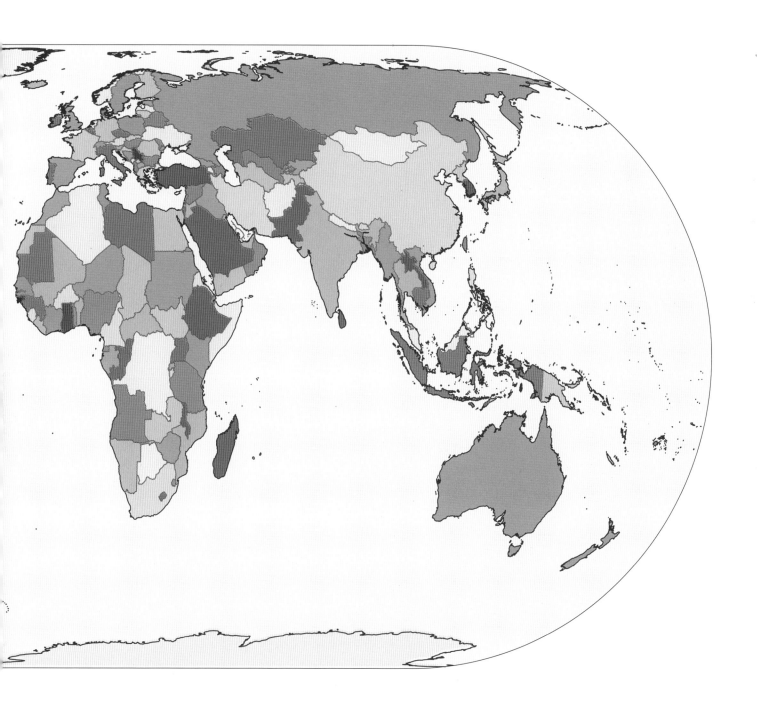

The United States is a very large country. It is divided into 50 smaller areas called states. Forty-eight of these states together cover one huge area of land. Two states, Alaska and Hawaii, are not part of this huge area.

Look at this map of the United States. Then answer the questions below. You can ask an adult for help.

Do you live in the United States? If you do, color in your state.

If you don't live in the United States, which state would you most like to visit? Color it in.

What is the name of the state you colored? Say the name aloud.

Some states, such as Texas, are very big. Other states, such as Rhode Island, are very small.

The United States is such a large country that it touches two oceans: the Pacific Ocean and the Atlantic Ocean. Many of the states in the United States also touch an ocean.

Look at the map of the United States below. Then color the Atlantic Ocean, the Pacific Ocean, and the Gulf of Mexico blue. Put an X (✗) on a state that touches one of these oceans. Is this the state where you live? Is this a state you have visited? You may ask an adult to help you.

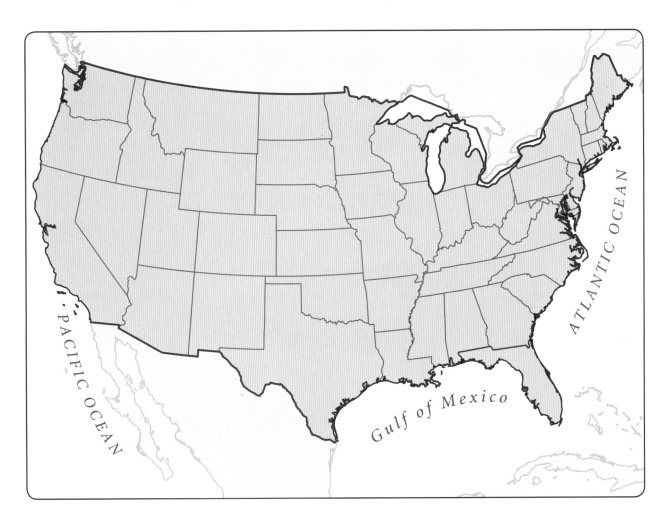

PACIFIC OCEAN

ATLANTIC OCEAN

Gulf of Mexico

How many US states have you visited? Point to them on the map. You may ask an adult to help you.

A city is a place that is full of office buildings, houses, parks, and schools. Large numbers of people live in cities. There are several large cities in most states.

Do you live in a city? What is the name of your city? Here are some pictures of things you might see in a city. Point to them and say what they are.

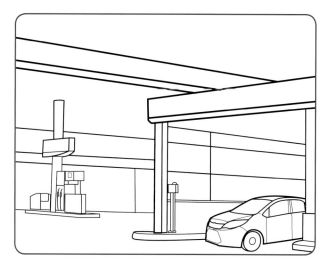

★ Your Neighborhood

The part of a city or town that is close to your home is called your neighborhood. The stores you use and your school are likely to be in your neighborhood. Many of the people you know probably live in your neighborhood.

Do you have friends in your neighborhood?
Draw a picture of something you like that is near your home.

Some places are much bigger than other places. A continent is bigger than the countries inside it. A country, such as the United States, is bigger than the states in it. A state is bigger than the cities in it. But cities are bigger than neighborhoods.

Look at these five different places. Can you number them in order of their size, from big to small? Start by putting a "1" next to the biggest place.

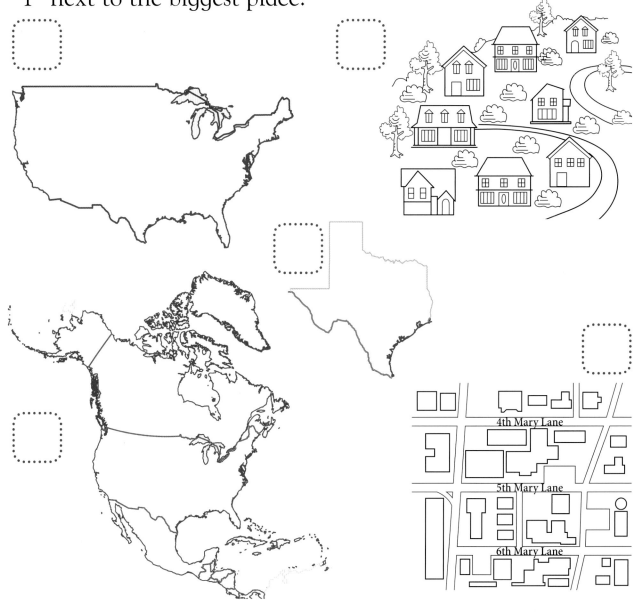

★ Map Keys

FACTS

A map uses symbols to tell you what you can find in a place. These symbols are explained in the map's key. A map's key lists all the symbols that are found on the map. It also tells you what each symbol represents.

Look at the pictures and map symbols below. Draw a line from each symbol to the picture of the thing it represents.

When you visit the zoo, you could lose your way without a map to help you. A zoo map, together with the symbols and pictures in the map's key, tells you which animals you can see at the zoo and where to find them.

Here is a map of a zoo with its key. Point to the symbol and picture of each animal in the key. Then point to where that animal is on the map.

Key

★ City Map

FACTS

A map of a city is very useful. It helps you find your way around the city. A city map tells you what places you can visit in the city and which streets you take to reach them.

Here is a map of some city streets. Some buildings have symbols on them. Find these buildings on the map and draw a circle around each of them. Then use the key to identify them. Point to each building and say what it is aloud.

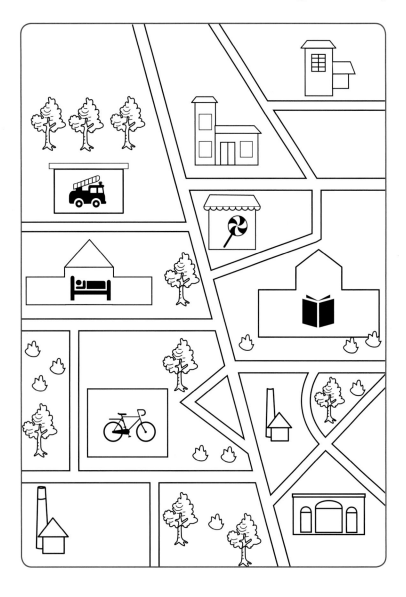

Key

library

candy store

fire department

bike shop

hotel

Some parks are large and include many different activities for you to enjoy. A park map and its key tell you what these activities are and where you can find them.

Here is a map of a park with its key. Point to where each place listed in the key is on the map, and say its name aloud.

Key

playground

sand box

picnic area

parking lot

A nature map helps you explore the natural world. If you go for a hike in the countryside, it will show you where natural features, such as rivers, lakes, forests, and mountains, are in the area.

Here is a map of a nature park with its key. Use the key to identify the different features from the natural world on the map. Point to them and say what they are aloud. Are there things from the human world on the map? Point to them and say what they are.

Key

campsite

lake

hills

forest

If you do not know where to go or what to do in a new place, you may need a map. The kind of map you need will depend on the kind of places you want to go.

Draw a line between the reason you need a map and the map that would help you the most.

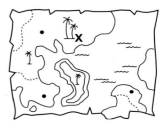

To find buried treasure

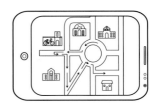

To see how Earth really looks

To drive to another city to visit your aunt and uncle

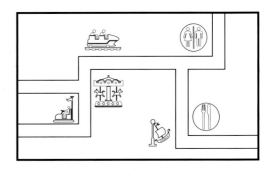

To go from the roller coaster to a restaurant in an amusement park

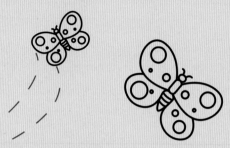

Certificate

Congratulations to

....

for successfully finishing this book.

pre-K Grade

GOOD JOB!

You're a star.

Date

....

Answer Section with Parents' Notes

This book is intended to support the geography concepts taught to your child in pre-kindergarten grade. It includes activities that test your child's knowledge of the world around him or her. By working through this book, your child will learn basic geography concepts in a fun and informative way.

Contents

These activities are intended to be completed by a child with adult support. The topics covered are as follows:
• The Earth and the solar system;
• Globes and maps;
• Types of map;
• Directions;
• The compass rose;
• The natural world and the human world;
• Landforms, such as mountains, deserts, islands, and forests;
• Bodies of water, such as oceans, lakes, and rivers;
• Continents, countries, and states;
• Cities and neighborhoods.

How to Help Your Child

As you work through the pages with your child, make sure he or she understands what each activity requires. Read the facts and instructions aloud. Encourage questions and reinforce observations that will build confidence and increase active participation in school.

By working with your child, you will understand how he or she thinks and learns. When appropriate, use props and objects from daily life to help your child make connections with the world outside.

If an activity is too challenging for your child, encourage him or her to try another page. Give encouragement by praising progress made as a correct answer is given and a page is completed. Good luck and remember to have fun!

★ Geography

FACTS

Geography is about the world and the way we use it. People who study geography are called geographers. Geographers study natural things, such as mountains and rivers. They also study things that people have added to the world, such as bridges and roads.

Look at the pictures below of four things a geographer might study. Say their names aloud. Circle the two pictures that show natural things.

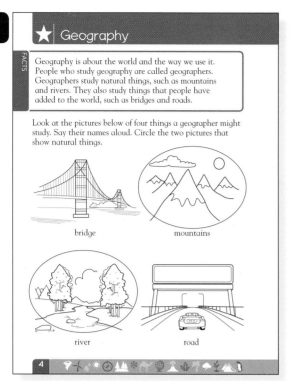

bridge   mountains

river   road

Ask your child why he or she thinks it might be interesting to learn about the world around you. Encourage your child to share questions or thoughts he or she has about the subject to begin to spark an interest in geography and make connections to his or her interests.

Planet Earth ★

FACTS

The planet we live on is called Earth. It is round like a ball. Earth moves around the sun. The sun provides Earth with heat and light.

Point to each picture below of things that you find on Earth. Say the name aloud as you point.

volcano   buildings

trees   island

Talk to your child about why it is important to take care of the Earth. Is your child aware that it is the only planet where humans can live! Clean air, water, and soil are important for every living creature. Talk about ways you and your family can help to take care of the Earth.

★ Earth and the Solar System

FACTS

Earth is a planet that moves around our sun. Other planets also move around our sun. The sun and the planets that travel around it make up our solar system.

Here is a picture of our solar system. Earth is the third planet from the sun. Find Earth and circle it.

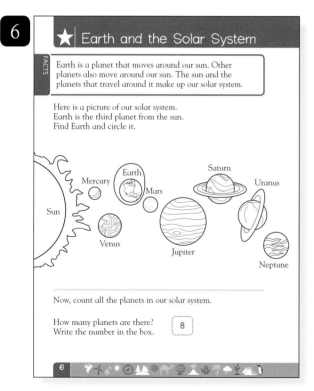

Sun   Mercury   Earth   Mars   Saturn   Uranus
Venus   Jupiter   Neptune

Now, count all the planets in our solar system.

How many planets are there? Write the number in the box.   8

One reason why Earth is a good place for people is that it is just the right distance from the sun to allow us to live at comfortable temperatures. Ask your child to point to the planets where it would be too hot or too cold to live.

Globes ★

FACTS

A globe is a map of planet Earth. It is shaped like a ball, just like Earth. This shape is called a sphere. A globe gives a very real picture of what our planet looks like.

Look at the picture below. How many globes and spheres can you spot? Point to each of them and say the word "globe" or "sphere" aloud.

Invite your child to look around your home to find more items that are shaped like a globe (spheres). Have your child describe to you what he or she notices about spheres.

8

★ Looking at a Globe

A globe is made to look just like our planet Earth. Like Earth, it is a sphere. On the outside of a globe are pictures of all the land and water on Earth. Globes are often made so that they can spin around. That's because Earth spins around in space.

On this globe, draw an arrow that goes from one side of Earth to the other. Then stand up and spin around in a complete circle, just like Earth does every day!

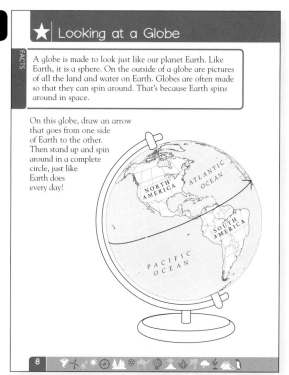

If you have a globe at home, bring it out and allow your child to explore it. Encourage your child to point out features on the globe that he or she notices. Point out where you live. If you do not have a globe at home, try your local library.

9

Globes and Flat Maps ★

A map is a kind of picture that shows you how to get to a place and find your way around it. Globes are maps that have the same shape as Earth. But you can also use a flat map to show places on Earth. Flat maps are easier to hold and use than a globe. You can look at a flat map on paper or on a screen.

Look at the pictures below. Point to each one and say if it is a flat map or a globe.

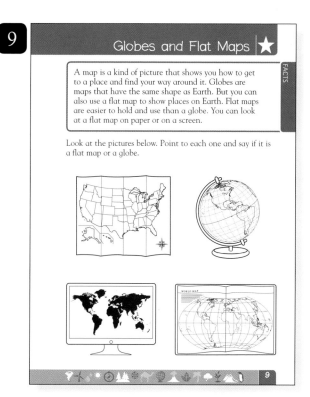

Tell your child how and when you use maps in your daily life. Give examples of common maps you use, and whether you use paper maps, electronic maps, or both. When you next use a map, invite your child to read the map with you.

10

★ Types of Map

There are many different types of map. This is because we use different maps for different reasons. If you were going on a hike in a nature park, you would need a map of the park. If you wanted to know the way around your neighborhood, you would need a map of your neighborhood.

Point to the map shown below that you would use to:

1. see the real shape of Earth
2. find the best road to your friend's house
3. find buried treasure
4. find your way around a nature park

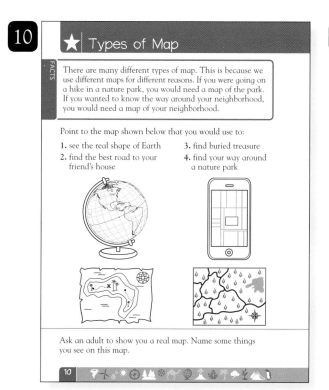

Ask an adult to show you a real map. Name some things you see on this map.

Together, look at a map that you commonly use. Ask your child which picture on page 10 looks most like this map. Ask your child what he or she sees on the map, and explain to your child how you use this map.

Directions ★

Directions are instructions that tell you where places or things are located. Using directions with a map can tell you exactly how to get from one place to another.

Look at the picture below. The cat, the dog, and the bird each have to go in a different direction to reach the house. Use your finger to trace a path from each animal to the house. Use one of the words in the box to describe the direction each animal takes.

up
across
down

Extend the activity using a toy. Place the toy in different spots in relation to your child, and have him or her state whether the toy is above, next to, or across from him or her.

★ Up and Down

"Up" and "down" are direction words that can tell you where something is, or where something is going. When something goes up, it moves to a higher place. When something goes down, it moves to a lower position.

Look at the picture of the house above. Read the sentences below. Circle "UP" or "DOWN" to say whether the object in each sentence is UPstairs or DOWNstairs.

The bathtub is UP / DOWN.

The cat is UP / DOWN.

The round table is UP / DOWN.

Ask your child to look around and point to and name things that are up above him or her. Then ask your child to point out things that are down below him or her.

In and Out ★

"In" and "out" are direction words that can tell you where you may put something or find something. You may put your books and pencils into a backpack so you can carry them to school. In class, you may take them out of your backpack so you can use them.

Draw lines from the backpack to the things that you can carry in it. Put an X (✗) over the objects that you cannot carry in the backpack.

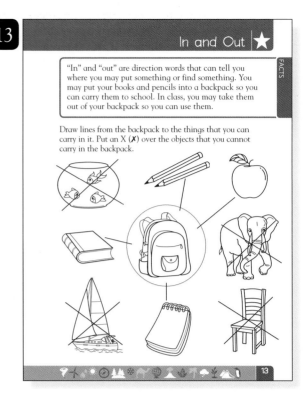

With your child, think of things that go in and out. For example, you might take a container of milk out of the refrigerator, and then put it back in. Together, come up with as many in-and-out examples as you can.

★ Near and Far

"Near" and "far" are direction words that tell you whether things are close together or not. Your pillow, for example, is usually near your bed but far from the bathtub. Remember that "near" and "far" can describe a very wide range of different distances. You may say that you live far from your friend. But if you think about how far you both are from the moon, you really live very near each other!

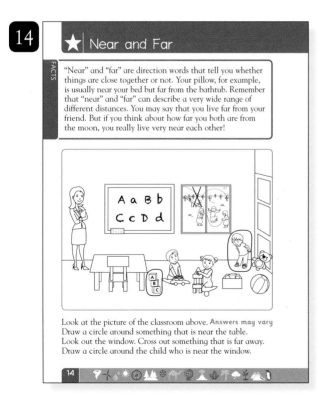

Look at the picture of the classroom above. Answers may vary
Draw a circle around something that is near the table.
Look out the window. Cross out something that is far away.
Draw a circle around the child who is near the window.

Ask your child whether places he or she knows are near or far from your home, and to explain the answer. For example, your child may say the library is near you, because you can walk there, but say Grandpa lives far away, because you have to drive to his house.

Above and Below ★

"Above" and "below" are direction words that are used to tell you whether something is higher or lower than another thing. Birds in the trees, for example, are above your head, while worms in the dirt are below your feet. Also, you are above the worms and below the birds.

Look at the picture above. Then circle "ABOVE" or "BELOW" to complete these sentences.

The teddy bear is ABOVE / BELOW the car.

The drum is ABOVE / BELOW the robot.

The castle is ABOVE / BELOW the airplane.

Play a guessing game with your child using the directions "above" and "below." For example, say "I see something blue below the chair." to your child. He or she must then guess the item. Take turns giving above and below clues.

★ Left and Right

FACTS

"Left" and "right" are direction words that you use based on where you are standing. If something is on the same side of you as your right hand, you say it is on your right. Something on the same side of you as your left hand is on your left.

Pretend it is you in the picture below. Hold up both your thumbs and point your fingers as shown. Put an **L** in the box next to the animals that are on your left. Put an **R** in the box next to the animals that are on your right.

Sometimes, children have a hard time remembering left from right. To help reinforce the concepts, use the directions "left" and "right" often in conversation with your child. For example, when traveling in the car, you might say, "Now we're turning left onto Maple Street."

Neighborhood Directions ★

FACTS

You can use direction words to tell visitors how to reach your house and find their way around your neighborhood.

Walk around your neighborhood with an adult. Try and describe the route you take, using as many different direction words as you can remember.
Next, stand outside the front door of your home or building. Say what you see when you:

1. look up
2. look to the left
3. look to the right
4. look down

Draw one of the things you saw outside your door in the box below.

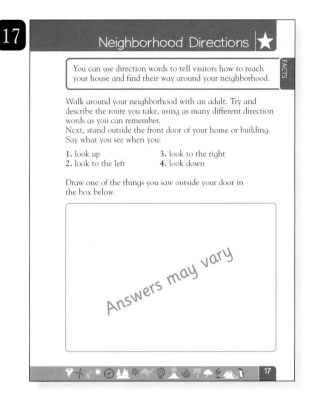

Answers may vary

Take a walk through your neighborhood. Describe your journey as you go along: "We are walking straight to the stop sign. Then we will turn right on First Street. We will pass the elementary school." This will help your child to get to know your neighborhood, while also reinforcing directions.

★ Map Directions

FACTS

You will also need to be familiar with direction words when following or describing a route on a map.

Look at this map of a playground. Then draw arrows on the map to show the route, described below, that Buster the dog takes when he visits the playground.

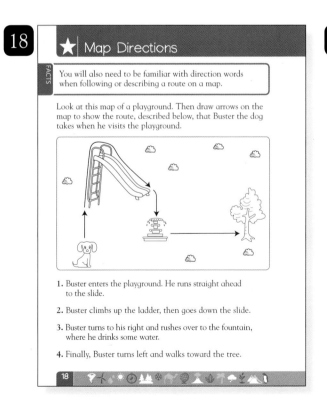

1. Buster enters the playground. He runs straight ahead to the slide.

2. Buster climbs up the ladder, then goes down the slide.

3. Buster turns to his right and rushes over to the fountain, where he drinks some water.

4. Finally, Buster turns left and walks toward the tree.

Reinforce this activity by playing a game of giving your child directions for moving around the house. For example, say, "Go around the chair, crawl under the table, turn left, and then go down the hall." Then switch, and have your child give you directions.

Compass Rose ★

FACTS

Most maps have something called a compass rose. Four main directions are marked on a compass rose: "north," "south," "east," and "west." On most maps, the direction "north" is at the top and the direction "south" is at the bottom.

Here is the compass rose. Look at the letters on it.

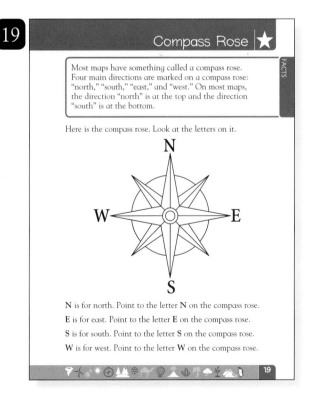

N is for north. Point to the letter **N** on the compass rose.

E is for east. Point to the letter **E** on the compass rose.

S is for south. Point to the letter **S** on the compass rose.

W is for west. Point to the letter **W** on the compass rose.

Find a map that you commonly use and ask your child to point out the compass rose on the map. Have him or her name the four directions on the rose.

★ North

The direction "north" is usually at the top of a map.

Here is a map of a city neighborhood. Put your finger on the fire department and move it in the direction of north. **Hint:** You are going north on the map when you move in the direction of NORTH on the compass rose.

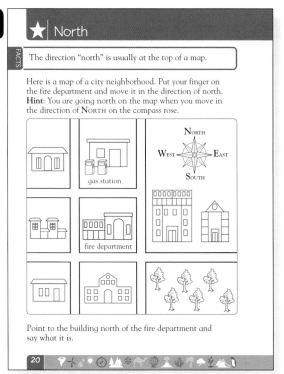

Point to the building north of the fire department and say what it is.

Find a map of your area. Point out your town or neighborhood. With your child, point out some places that lie north of where you live. Support your child as necessary in reading the names of these places.

South ★

The direction "south" is usually at the bottom of a map.

Look at the map of a bedroom below. Put your finger on the south wall. Say what piece of furniture is next to this wall. **Hint:** You are going south on the map when you move in the direction of SOUTH on the compass rose.

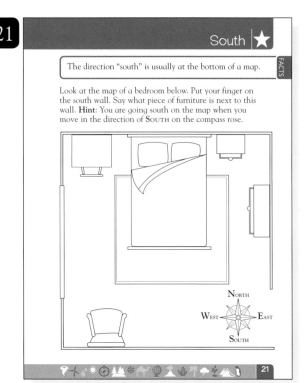

Find a map of your area. Point out your town or neighborhood. With your child, point out some places that lie south of where you live. Support your child as necessary in reading the names of these places.

★ East

The direction "east" is usually on the right side of a map.

Here is a map of a lake. You are helping the fish find its way. Can you say which animal is east of the fish?

Find a map of your area. Point out your town or neighborhood. With your child, point out some places that lie east of where you live. Support your child as necessary in reading the names of these places.

West ★

The direction "west" is usually on the left side of a map.

Here is a map of a zoo showing the animals that live there. Say which animal you will find to the west of the main building.

Find a map of your area. Point out your town or neighborhood. With your child, point out some places that that lie west of where you live. Support your child as necessary in reading the names of these places.

★ The Natural World

There are two different ways to think about the world. People study the natural world, and they also study the human world. Animals, plants, land, and water are all part of the natural world. They were on the planet before people started adding things to the world.

Here is a picture of a beach. Color the things that are part of the natural world. Circle the things that are part of the human world.

Take a look around you. What things can you and your child see that are part of the natural world? Name them. Help him or her distinguish things that are part of the natural world from things that are part of the human world.

The Human World ★

People create all kinds of things to make their lives easier. They construct roads and bridges to help them cross rivers and mountains. They build towns and cities, where they live. Anything made by people is part of the human world.

Play an "I Spy" game with your child, where you take turns guessing items you see around you from the human world or the natural world. Lead off each round with "I spy something from the human world." That is the first clue!

★ Mountains

Mountains are high areas of land. A group of mountains together is called a mountain range.

Look at this map of the continent of North America. Circle the three mountain ranges that you see on it.

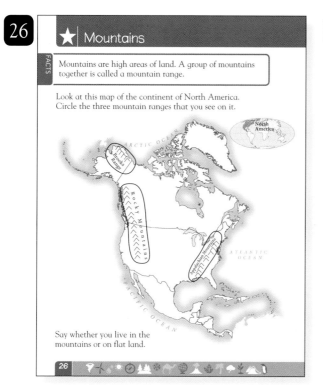

Say whether you live in the mountains or on flat land.

Look up pictures online of some of the world's famous mountains and mountain ranges, such as Mount Everest or the Rocky Mountains. Have your child describe these mountains to you in his or her own words.

Forests ★

Forests are places with lots of trees. The trees give forest animals food and protection. The animals eat leaves, nuts, berries, and seeds. They may climb the trees and hide in the branches or dig holes to stay safe.

Circle all the forest animals you can find.

Tell your child that forests are often shown in green on maps. Point out a forest on a map. Even better, if you live near a forest, take your child on a walk through it to experience it firsthand.

★ Deserts

FACTS

The driest places on Earth are called deserts. Deserts get very little rain. That is why you will not find very many plants growing in a desert.

You are going on vacation to a desert, where the sun is always shining. It gets very hot. Circle the things you will want to pack for your trip. Put an X (✗) on the items that you would not pack.

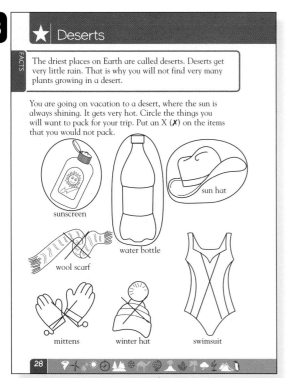

sunscreen

water bottle

sun hat

wool scarf

mittens

winter hat

swimsuit

Help your child visualize deserts by looking online to find pictures of some of the world's most well-known deserts, such as the Sahara in Africa. Your child might be interested to know that Antarctica, which is one of the coldest places on Earth, is also a desert, because it has almost no rainfall.

Islands ★

FACTS

An island is a piece of land that is surrounded by water. Islands look like they are floating in water, but they are not. Islands are the tops of mountains, most of which are under the water.

The map below shows the main islands of the state of Hawaii in the United States. Count them, then say how many there are. Color in the largest island.

Draw a boat that can help people go from one island to another.

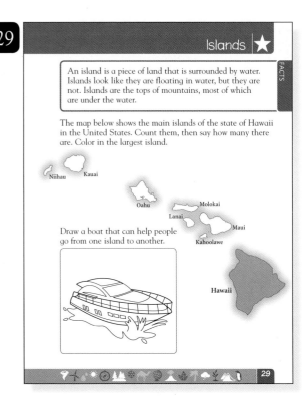

Niihau   Kauai

Oahu

Molokai

Lanai

Maui

Kahoolawe

Hawaii

Explain that islands can be very large or very small. Greenland, in the North Atlantic Ocean, is one of the world's largest islands. Nauru, in the South Pacific Ocean, is the world's smallest island nation. Look on a map to find islands of different sizes to compare.

★ Oceans

FACTS

An ocean is a very, very large body of water. Did you know that oceans take up more space on Earth than land? There are five oceans. They cover most of our planet. It is hard to see where one ocean starts and the other ends, because all oceans touch one another.

Look at the map below. Circle the names of the five oceans. Then answer the questions that follow.

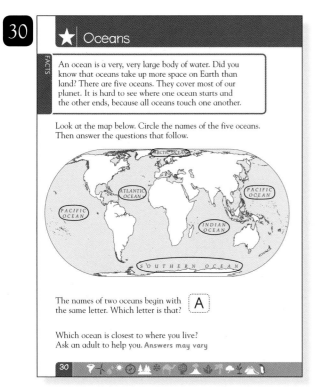

ARCTIC OCEAN

ATLANTIC OCEAN

PACIFIC OCEAN

PACIFIC OCEAN

INDIAN OCEAN

SOUTHERN OCEAN

The names of two oceans begin with the same letter. Which letter is that?   A

Which ocean is closest to where you live?
Ask an adult to help you. Answers may vary

Ask your child if he or she can name the ocean that is closest to where you live. Look on a map together to check his or her answer or to find the answer.

Lakes ★

FACTS

A lake is a body of water surrounded by land. Lakes are much smaller than oceans. People like to live around lakes, where they can fish, swim, and go boating.

The pictures below show different things you might use to cross a lake. Point to each one and say its name aloud. Have you used any of these to cross a lake?

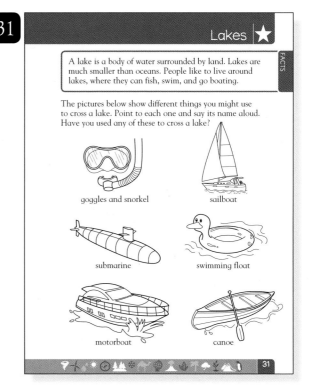

goggles and snorkel

sailboat

submarine

swimming float

motorboat

canoe

Ask your child if lakes are part of the human or the natural world. Then explain that some lakes are natural, and others have been created by people. Lakes are often formed when dams are built across rivers. For example, Lake Livingston in Texas was created in this way.

★ Rivers

A river is a body of water that moves from a high place to a low place. Often rivers run down the sides of mountains. Many people and animals live near rivers.

In this picture, find five living things that are using the river. Point to them and say their names aloud.

Look at a map to find the river nearest to your home. Find out what happens along that river, either by visiting it or going online for information. Do people use it mostly for fun (fishing, swimming, boating) or for other purposes, such as moving things from place to place?

Continents ★

There are seven very large areas of land on Earth. These large areas of land are called continents. Asia is the largest continent. Australia is the smallest continent. Antarctica is covered with ice all year round.

Here is a flat map of the world. Color in all of the land.
Remember: Everything you do not color on this map is water.

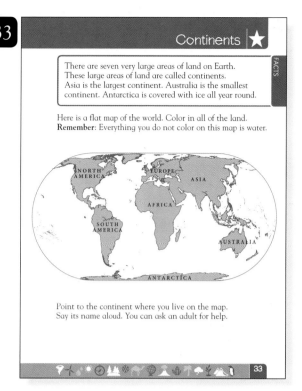

Point to the continent where you live on the map. Say its name aloud. You can ask an adult for help.

Together, find the continent where you live and point to it on the map. You might also tell your child that no one lives permanently on the continent of Antarctica. Scientists work there, but return home after they have spent some time there.

★ Countries

Continents are divided into places called countries. Continents are part of the natural world, but countries are part of the human world.

Look at this map of the world. Then answer the questions below. Ask an adult to help you.

What is the name of the country where you live?
...... Answers may vary ......

Can you find it on the world map? Point to it and say the name aloud.
Answers may vary

Can you point to Canada and Russia on the map? Circle them.

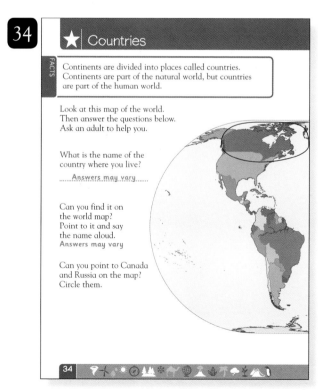

Talk to your child about what other countries people in your family have come from or lived in. Point these countries out on the map, and discuss how they are similar to or different from where you live.

Countries ★

Countries can be large or small. People living in the same country have the same leaders and the same flag. The two largest countries on Earth are Russia and Canada.

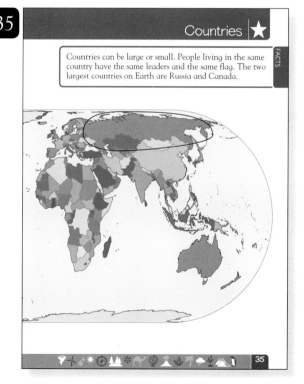

Your child might be curious about how many countries are in the world. There are 196. If he or she would like to learn more about another country, visit a library to find a book with information about that country, or perhaps a storybook that is set in that country.

★ States

FACTS

The United States is a very large country. It is divided into 50 smaller areas called states. Forty-eight of these states together cover one huge area of land. Two states, Alaska and Hawaii, are not part of this huge area.

Look at this map of the United States. Then answer the questions below. You can ask an adult for help. **Answers may vary**

Do you live in the United States? If you do, color in your state.

If you don't live in the United States, which state would you most like to visit? Color it in.

What is the name of the state you colored? Say the name aloud.

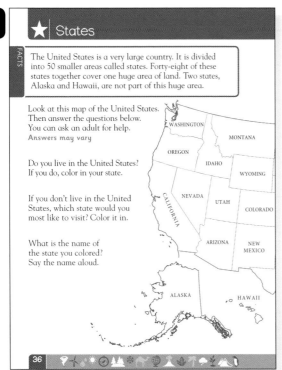

Create personal connections to the map of the United States. If you live in the United States, point out your state on the map and talk about its landscape or weather. Discuss places you have visited. If you don't live in the US, you could talk about a state that you would like to visit.

States ★

FACTS

Some states, such as Texas, are very big. Other states, such as Rhode Island, are very small.

Use the map to review and reinforce the four directions. Point to the state of Kansas in the center of the United States. Then ask your child to point to the states that lie to the north, south, east, and west of Kansas. Say the names of these states aloud as your child points to them.

★ Finding States

FACTS

The United States is such a large country that it touches two oceans: the Pacific Ocean and the Atlantic Ocean. Many of the states in the United States also touch an ocean.

Look at the map of the United States below. Then color the Atlantic Ocean, the Pacific Ocean, and the Gulf of Mexico blue. Put an X (✗) on a state that touches one of these oceans. Is this the state where you live? Is this a state you have visited? You may ask an adult to help you. **Answers may vary**

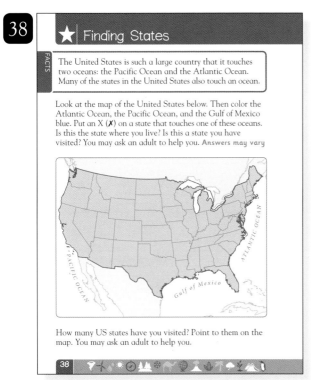

How many US states have you visited? Point to them on the map. You may ask an adult to help you.

Reinforce directions further by asking your child which ocean lies to the east of the United States and which lies to the west. Also, if you live in the US, ask your child which of these two oceans is closer to your home state.

Cities ★

FACTS

A city is a place that is full of office buildings, houses, parks, and schools. Large numbers of people live in cities. There are several large cities in most states.

Do you live in a city? What is the name of your city? Here are some pictures of things you might see in a city. Point to them and say what they are. **Answers may vary**

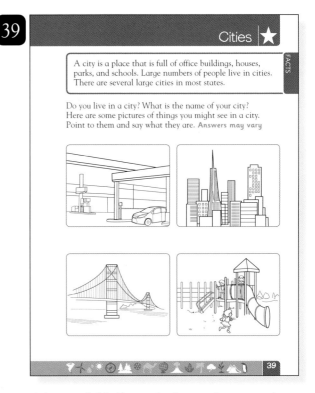

Ask your child if he or she knows the name of the biggest city in your state. It may be where you live! Find a map of your area or state and point out this city on the map. Also, point out other cities in your state, especially ones you and your child have visited or are near your home.

★ Your Neighborhood

FACTS

The part of a city or town that is close to your home is called your neighborhood. The stores you use and your school are likely to be in your neighborhood. Many of the people you know probably live in your neighborhood.

Do you have friends in your neighborhood?
Draw a picture of something you like that is near your home.

Answers may vary

Ask your child to imagine that an alien has landed in your neighborhood and wants to learn about it. How would your child describe your neighborhood? What parts of the neighborhood would he or she want to mention to someone who is unfamiliar with it?

What's Bigger? ★

FACTS

Some places are much bigger than other places. A continent is bigger than the countries inside it. A country, such as the United States, is bigger than the states in it. A state is bigger than the cities in it. But cities are bigger than neighborhoods.

Look at these five different places. Can you number them in order of their size, from big to small? Start by putting a "1" next to the biggest place.

2 5
3
1 4

Extend the activity by having your child point out two sections on a globe or map and asking you which is bigger. He or she will gain confidence by being the "teacher" who knows the answer!

★ Map Keys

FACTS

A map uses symbols to tell you what you can find in a place. These symbols are explained in the map's key. A map's key lists all the symbols that are found on the map. It also tells you what each symbol represents.

Look at the pictures and map symbols below. Draw a line from each symbol to the picture of the thing it represents.

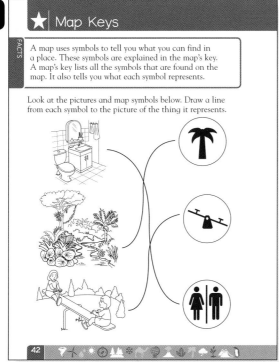

Find a map you commonly use and ask your child to find the key. Point out each symbol on the key and name what it stands for. Encourage your child to find each symbol on the map.

Zoo Map ★

FACTS

When you visit the zoo, you could lose your way without a map to help you. A zoo map, together with the symbols and pictures in the map's key, tells you which animals you can see at the zoo and where to find them.

Here is a map of a zoo with its key. Point to the symbol and picture of each animal in the key. Then point to where that animal is on the map.

Key

Many zoos post their maps online. With your child, look at some examples of zoo maps and talk about what information they offer. Does a zoo seem large or small from its map? What animals are there? What else do any of the maps show you, besides the types of animals that are kept there?

★ City Map

A map of a city is very useful. It helps you find your way around the city. A city map tells you what places you can visit in the city and which streets you take to reach them.

Here is a map of some city streets. Some buildings have symbols on them. Find these buildings on the map and draw a circle around each of them. Then use the key to identify them. Point to each building and say what it is aloud.

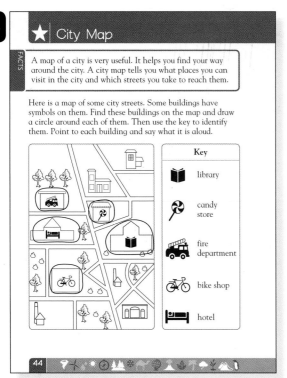

Encourage your child to use a crayon to trace routes on the map between different points. For example, have him or her trace a route between the fire department and the bike shop.

Park Map ★

Some parks are large and include many different activities for you to enjoy. A park map and its key tell you what these activities are and where you can find them.

Here is a map of a park with its key. Point to where each place listed in the key is on the map, and say its name aloud.

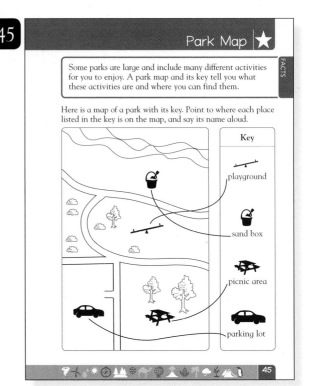

Explain to your child that park maps are often displayed at the entrance to a park, and sometimes in other places around the park. A park map usually shows the spot where the person looking at it is standing. Point out maps to your child when you next visit a park.

★ Nature Map

A nature map helps you explore the natural world. If you go for a hike in the countryside, it will show you where natural features, such as rivers, lakes, forests, and mountains, are in the area.

Here is a map of a nature park with its key. Use the key to identify the different features from the natural world on the map. Point to them and say what they are aloud. Are there things from the human world on the map? Point to them and say what they are.

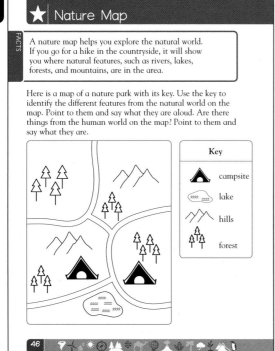

Tell your child that the way some maps are drawn makes them very beautiful objects. Find some examples, if you can, to show your child. Encourage your child to turn the map on this page into a work of art by adding to it in any way he or she would like.

Which Map? ★

If you do not know where to go or what to do in a new place, you may need a map. The kind of map you need will depend on the kind of places you want to go.

Draw a line between the reason you need a map and the map that would help you the most.

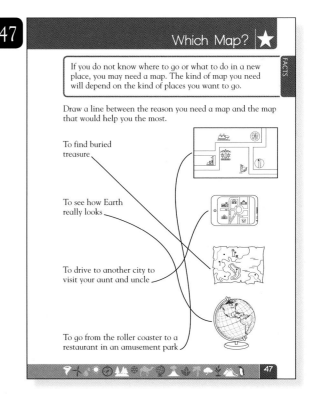

Ask your child to talk about possible situations when someone might need to use the various maps shown on this page. Let your child take the lead, with you filling in any extra details where necessary.